CLASSIC AUSTRALIA

Spectacular Panoramic Views

Australia's treasure lies in its superb natural heritage. In the red-dust deserts of the Outback, or along the beaches of Australia's sun-soaked north, we draw close to the living heart of a remarkable land.

Australia is frontier country, where people may still walk freely amid pristine wilderness, feeling its power and majesty. Under the rainforest canopies and the immense desert sky, beside still pools and flowing waterfalls, the natural world casts its illuminating light upon our own lives.

When we reflect on the beauty of God's creation, we are better able to put things in perspective. Our own lives are truly small compared with the vast world around us. We are linked with this land. If we take the time to enjoy it, it will nourish our souls.

TITLE PAGE
Majestic Uluru, Northern Territory

LEFT
Whitehaven Beach, Queensland

Ken Duncan was born in Mildura, Victoria, in 1954. A professional photographer since 1980, his work has received many industry awards both in Australia and overseas, and he is now recognized as one of the world's leading panoramic landscape specialists. Typically casual about such accolades, Ken prefers to say he is just an average photographer with a mighty God. His goal and passion in life is simply to show people the beauty of God's creation, encouraging them to look beyond themselves to something far greater. Enjoy the journey as you wander with Ken through the pages of this book, experiencing the wonder of an amazing continent.

RIGHT
Hopetoun Falls, Victoria

PREVIOUS PAGE
Kimberley Boabs, Derby, Western Australia

LEFT
Upolu Cay, Cairns, Queensland

RIGHT
Face of the Ages,
The Twelve Apostles, Victoria

NEXT PAGE
Russell Falls, Tasmania

ABOVE
Normanton Railway, Queensland

ABOVE
Richmond Bridge, Tasmania

Like a beacon of hope in an endless sea of desert, Uluru glows in the rays of the setting sun. Monumental in proportion, it is one of the world's great natural monoliths, commanding the surrounding plain on every side.

For the indigenous landowners, Uluru is the source of all dreams. For others, it is an awesome display of God's creative power. For still others, it is a geological marvel that begs to be seen and photographed.

There will always be differing opinions. The test for us as a nation is whether we can stand together in unity in spite of our differences. In the end, it's how we accept one another that proves who we really are.

LEFT
Timeless Land, Uluru, Northern Territory

Rising jewel-like from the Great Southern Ocean, remote Lucky Bay greets the weary traveller along Western Australia's south coast.

For those who have journeyed across the barren Nullarbor and the vast rural reaches of the state's south-east, Lucky Bay is like a paradise in waiting. Everything is prepared — a path through the dunes, a sweep of white sand, a gentle surf lapping the shore, a sea of brilliant aquas and deep cool blues.

Arriving here makes everything that has been endured along the way seem worth while. We all need time in places like this, where we may wash away the anxieties of the world and be refreshed once more for the journey ahead.

RIGHT
Lucky Bay, Western Australia

RIGHT
Rising Force, The Skillion, Terrigal, New South Wales

LEFT
Coffin Bay National Park, South Australia

NEXT PAGE
Piccaninny Creek, Purnululu National Park, Western Australia

LEFT
Natural Arch, Queensland

RIGHT
*Refuge Cove,
Wilsons Promintory, Victoria*

ABOVE
Petrol Bowser, Silverton, New South Wales

ABOVE
Pinnacles, Western Australia

LEFT
Arkaba Woolshed, Flinders Ranges, South Australia

RIGHT
North Beach, Lord Howe Island, New South Wales

Flowing like silk, the gently stepped waters of Cephissus Falls murmur between mossed banks and dwarf-like pandini trees. The forest stretches into the stillness on either side. Not far away, massive Huon Pines – some dating back to the very time of Christ – tower over the valley that has taken their name.

We desperately need to preserve more special places like this. They are sanctuaries from the storms of our modern lives, pockets of Eden where we may walk more closely with our Creator.

Time is short. Unless we act now to protect the last remnants of Earth's ancient forests, there will be precious little left for succeeding generations.

LEFT
Living Waters, Pine Valley, Tasmania

The early settlers were a hardy breed. Those who came to this region of South Australia were ex Diggers, awarded grants of land following the First World War. They were tough, resourceful people, independent-minded and inured to hardship after the bitter experiences of the battlefield.

This house stands as a testimony to one man's effort in taming a difficult land. Empty now, left abandoned in a field, the memories and stories yet linger.

How much we take for granted in our convenience-based society. These people fought to provide even the smallest comfort for their families. Can we learn from their example?

RIGHT
Forgotten Dreams, Burra, South Australia

PREVIOUS PAGE
Sunset, Haasts Bluff, Northern Territory

RIGHT
Hill Inlet, Whitsunday Island, Queensland

LEFT
On the Road to Gundagai, New South Wales

ABOVE
The Remarkables, Kangaroo Island, South Australia

ABOVE
Eucla, Western Australia

RIGHT
Kata Tjuta Country, Northern Territory

LEFT

Peace in the Valley, Ebor Falls, New South Wales

RIGHT
Echo Camp Waterhole, Arkaroola, South Australia

LEFT
The Labyrinth, Lake Elysia, Tasmania

On the Atherton Tablelands, the tropical rains feed innumerable waterfalls. Here, a brilliant white curtain of falling water contrasts with the shadowed depths of the forest and the vivid green tree ferns bursting from the volcanic soil. The air itself is charged with moisture, the dampness part of the very fabric of the forest. Water always reminds me of God's love for us — pure, freely given, unconditional, utterly life-giving. It always nourishes. It always causes growth. Just like the rain pouring into the rainforest, God's love brings life and healing to all who draw from it.

PREVIOUS PAGE
Broad Horizons, Craig's Hut, Alpine National Park, Victoria

LEFT
Millaa Millaa Falls, Queensland

In Kakadu, the close of the wet season makes for some beautiful photographs, and sometimes for some rather close encounters of the crocodilian kind!

Not realizing this, my companion and I headed straight for these falls and leapt in. As others wandered by, we wondered why no one else saw fit to join us in the water.

Leaving the park, we remarked how much we had enjoyed our swim.

The Ranger looked shocked. Hadn't we read the 'No Swimming!' signs in the camping ground? We admitted that we hadn't — that we had gone straight to the falls instead. Apparently a saltwater crocodile was still at large in the area. All efforts to trap it had failed. Praise God for looking after us! But how often it's like that in life — we are so focussed on our activities that we neglect the warning signs provided.

RIGHT
Jim Jim Falls, Kakadu, Northern Territory

LEFT
Walls of Jerusalem, Tasmania

RIGHT
Ancient Land, Geiki Gorge, Western Australia

ABOVE
Fern Gully, Triplet Falls, Victoria

ABOVE
Satin Waters, King George Falls, Western Australia

RIGHT
Champagne Pools, Fraser Island, Queensland

LEFT
Three Sisters, New South Wales

NEXT PAGE
Misty Morning, Strzelecki Ranges, Victoria

Tasmania is Australia's 'wild light' capital. Its constantly changing weather patterns are like an ever-turning kaleidoscope, filtering the light in all sorts of unpredictable ways. Photographers simply have to learn to wait for the right moment.

To get this shot we camped for two days on the top of Mount Amos, waiting for a break in the light. When it finally came we were rewarded with this awesome view of the Freycinet Peninsula and surrounding sea.

Patience is all about relaxing and enjoying the moment — entering into the rhythm of what is happening around you. Receiving what you've waited for is just an added bonus.

PREVIOUS PAGE
Peake Ruins, Oodnadatta, South Australia

RIGHT
Wine Glass Bay, Tasmania

To many, Australia is a desert continent — vast and arid, as barren as the rocks that break the surface of the land. For those with eyes to see, however, it is like a treasure, an immense expanse of ochred gold set with gemstones of amazing beauty.

As our journey comes to a close we stop at Wangi Falls, one of the jewels of Australia's Top End. Spring-fed and deliciously cool, the falls are a haven for visitors from Darwin. Pandanus palms burst upon the sultry air. The water tumbles down iron-strong cliffs. So many other gems are scattered through the pages of this book. I hope you have enjoyed the journey.

LEFT
Wangi Falls, Northern Territory

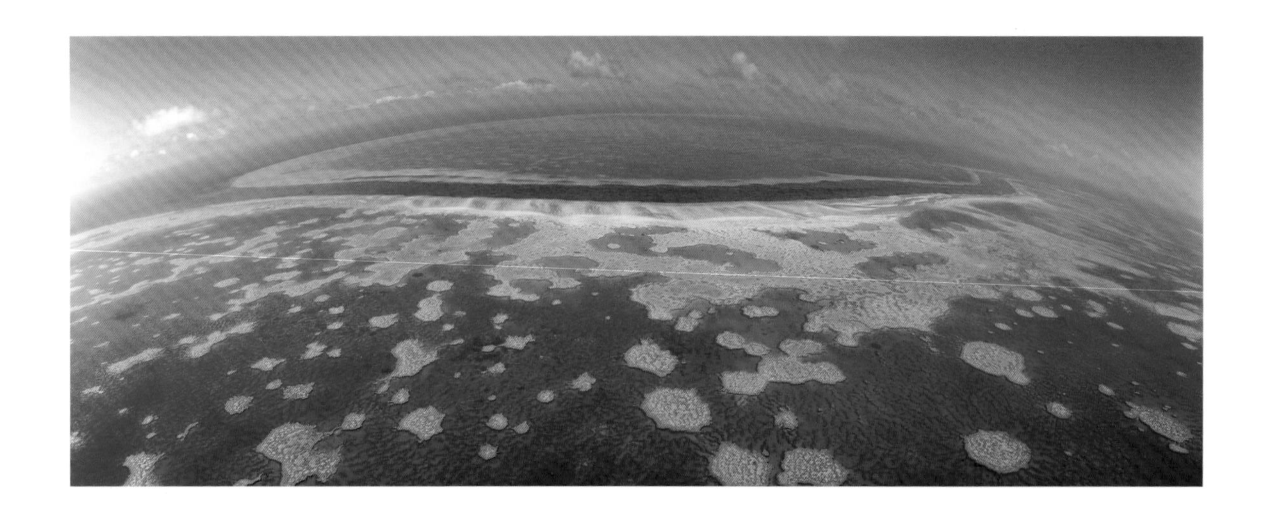

ABOVE
Great Barrier Reef, Queensland

CLASSIC AUSTRALIA
First published in 2002
Reprinted 2003 and 2004
by Ken Duncan Panographs®
Pty Limited
ABN 21 050 235 606
PO Box 3015, Wamberal
NSW 2260, Australia
Telephone +61 2 4367 6777
Email: panos@kenduncan.com

Designed by Good Catch Design
Edited by Peter Friend
Colour separations by
Digital Imaging Group
Printed and bound in China

The National Library of Australia
Cataloguing-in-Publication entry:
Duncan, Ken.
Classic Australia:
spectacular panoramic views.
ISBN 0 9577861 8 2.
1. Australia - Pictorial works. I. Title.
919.400222

To view the range of Ken Duncan's panoramic Limited Edition Prints visit our Galleries situated at:-

- 5740 Oak Road,
  Matcham, NSW
  Telephone +61 2 4367 6701
- 73 George Street,
  The Rocks, Sydney, NSW
  Telephone +61 2 9241 3460
- Shop U6 Southgate,
  Melbourne, VIC
  Telephone +61 3 9686 8022
- Shop 14
  Hunter Valley Gardens Village,
  Broke Road, Pokolbin, NSW
  Telephone +61 2 4998 6711

VISIT THE KEN DUNCAN GALLERY ON LINE: **www.kenduncan.com**